A SOLDIER'S THERAPEUTIC REFLECTIONS

James M. McMullan, Ed. S.

Copyright © 2024 James M. McMullan, Ed. S..

All rights reserved. No part of this book may be reproduced, stored, or transmitted by any means—whether auditory, graphic, mechanical, or electronic—without written permission of both publisher and author, except in the case of brief excerpts used in critical articles and reviews. Unauthorized reproduction of any part of this work is illegal and is punishable by law.

ISBN: 978-1-63950-243-1 (sc)
ISBN: 978-1-63950-244-8 (hc)
ISBN: 978-1-63950-245-5 (e)

This publication contains the opinions and ideas of its author. It is intended to provide helpful and informative material on the subjects addressed in the publication. The author and publisher specifically disclaim all responsibility for any liability, loss, or risk, personal or otherwise, which is incurred as a consequence, directly or indirectly, of the use and application of any of the contents of this book.

Writers Apex

Gateway Towards Success

8063 MADISON AVE #1252
Indianapolis, IN 46227
+13176596889
www.writersapex.com

Contents

Preface 1

"Expired Time in Service" 2

"Guard Duty" 3

"Transactions of Love" 4

"Breathe" 5

"The Game" 6

"Thoughts I received" 8

"Forever" 9

"Illusion" 10

"Love, Pain and Pleasure" 11

"Fathers, For Real" 12

"Twin Towers" 14

"Do Right Man" 16

"Unattached" 18

"The World In, Which We Live" 19

"The Why of Love" 21

"Fix It" 23

"He Was a Friend" 25

"If It Is Meant to Be" 27

Just Let It Be" 28

"Love Is" 29

"Man What a Lady" 30

"Our Love" 31

"Love Significance" 32

"Love's Journey" 33

"Questionable Friend" 34

"What You Think" 35

"Life" 36

"Come Back" 37

"I Need One More Day" 38

"We Sleep Alone" 39

"My Last Duty Station" 40

Preface

I began writing years ago as a method of relaxation and coping with everyday life situations. These writings are a reflection of my pain, my joy and my personal growth. I am pleased to share my writings with you.

Please read and enjoy.

Shout out to Doctor B. and Doctor J.

"Expired Time in Service"

I left my family and friends when I was only seventeen.

I found myself in a harsh military, an unknown scene.

Compared to my town, I found the world quite large.

I learned my mission and soon I was in charge.

I found myself terrified, waiting to go into a danger zone.

The young soldiers relied on me to set the tone.

Over twenty years have gone by and I am still nervous.

What will I do after my expired time in service?

James M. McMullan, Ed. S.

"Guard Duty"

Up on an empty and cold border.

Every sound is heard and it is getting colder.

The ammo bunker is long and shut tight.

The trees are slowly fading out of sight.

Three other soldiers pass me by, as we make it around.

The wind is blowing hard over the snow filled ground.

We are filled with a great sense of pride.

Greatly enduring the elements with our M16 by our side.

"Transactions of Love"

We meet a person to build a love and life with.

Listening and seeing people loving on must be a myth.

The rise and fall of those exciting times.

The things we did in private should be crimes.

The first few days of our love lead into a year.

You gave me your time and your love without fear.

I support you in everything you do.

You support me and love me too.

Being around you makes my heart as pure as a dove.

We give meaning to term "Transactions of Love".

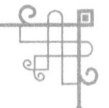

"Breathe"

I can not seem to get any unfiltered air.

The darkness is overwhelming and unfair.

My head is spinning out of control.

I hear the platoon sergeant yelling from my fox hole.

It is as if we have been here for years,
but it has only been days.

The cold air is sliding through like a haze.

The never ending wounds of military life is a disease.

The rain is falling harder and harder,
it is so difficult to breathe.

"The Game"

I do not understand the ways to be part of relationships.

Others have obtained the secret, but I
missed obtaining it somehow.

I feel as if I am not even in the game.

The relationship game is passing me by.

I am led to believe that I am plagued to be the referee.

I know the rules, but I am not allowed
to play, only referee.

I can see the joy and feel the excitement
of others as they play the game.

I can feel the joy and excitement, but
I cannot get into the game.

I take off my uniform and put my whistle on
the shelf, but my referee image remains.

James M. McMullan, Ed. S.

*In the relationship game, I guess I am
destined to play the part of the referee.*

*Others do not hesitate when asking for my help on
how to play the game, but they never ask me to play.*

My fellow referees see themselves as victims.

They do not understand their destiny.

*The joy and laughter astound me, and I
want so desperately to be in the game.*

*Looking out across the field as the game is
being played, I realize that I am a referee,
and I am part of the game too.*

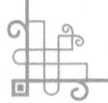

"Thoughts I received"

Do not spend major time with minor people. If there are people in your life that continually disappoint you, break promises, stomp on your dreams, being too judgmental, have different values and do not have your back during difficult times, that is not a friend. To have a friend is to be a friend. (That is a lesson you must learn and accept early in life if you want to be a part of someone). Sometimes in life as you grow, your friends will either grow with you or go. Surround yourself with people who reflect your values, goals, interests, and lifestyle. When I think of any of my successes, I am thankful to my family and friends that have enriched my life. Over the years my phone book has changed because I have changed for the better. At first, you think you're going to be alone, but after a while new people show up in your life that make your life so much sweeter and easier to endure. Remember, "Birds of a feather flock together." If you are an eagle, do not hang around with chickens: Chickens cannot fly and they try in every way to keep you down on the ground with them.

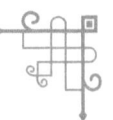

"Forever"

I am in this place, it is dark and I do not seem
to have much room, but it is secure.

I am safe here, forever.

I am down on my knees, but one day I
will walk just like them, I am sure.

Somehow, I know it is true because I
simply cannot crawl forever.

Where am I? Look at all those girls and boys!

I guess I will be fine, but I could not bring my toys!

Will I ever learn my ABC's, never.

Through the years I made A's not D's, I've worked
hard, and others think that I am clever.

Graduation day has come and gone, a
day I thought would never be.

Oh, to go back to that place where I was secure.

I think about that place, and I understand
the meaning of forever.

"Illusion"

Life appears to be in the midst of a cloud.

The sights and sounds aren't coming
in very clear or loud.

We did not take time yesterday. So we say, "Let us do
it tomorrow." But we never say, "Let us do it today."

Why not now? Would it bring sorrow
or is the price too high to pay?

World events at present make our outlook
on life a multitude of confusion.

We believe this in each and every way,
but this could all be an Illusion.

"Love, Pain and Pleasure"

Without the knowledge of pain, it is impossible
to appreciate a moment of pleasure.

Without the knowledge of distance,
it is impossible to measure.

My dreams became reality the
moment I knew and loved you.

Before my knowledge of you, I only knew pain.

With you, I began to experience pleasure.

I feel the joy of the sun on my face,
but I do not mind the rain.

The joy of love is important in any measure.

I feel as though I have been reborn.

You bring with you the joy of a rose
without the pain of its thorn.

"Fathers, For Real"

Fathers are men of misery when they are for real.

Fathers work hard at one job, sometimes
two in order to pay the bills.

Fathers fight harder than mothers to
be a part of their child's history.

Fathers work from sun up until sun
down in fields and mills.

Fathers struggle with the joys of love and home.

Fathers are the blame for all the hurt and pain.

Fathers never seem to be with their
children and they always roam.

Fathers are responsible for all the days filled with rain.

Fathers never let their children have fun.

Fathers are given the task of making everyone hardy.

*Fathers worry in the shadows while
mothers soak up the sun.*

*Fathers always fund the feast, but
they never get to the party.*

*Fathers are so misunderstood and never
seem to be a part of their child's life.*

Fathers are only called in times of despair.

*Fathers cannot be friends with their children,
they leave that to their wives.*

Fathers are men with a pure heart, soul and zeal.

When they are really doing their task, for real.

"Twin Towers"

The economy was bouncing back.

The stocks and bonds were on an upward track.

The GNP forecast had the best
results in quite some time.

Suddenly everything changed.

In the early morning hours, someone
from the East committed a crime.

Our nation suffered a terrible blow,
and our lives were rearranged.

Someone from the East said, "I will destroy
those Twin Towers in the West."

They viewed the Twin Towers as a source
of evil against everyone in the East.

One man viewed the Twin Towers
and influenced the rest.

People in the East view him as a leader, while those in the West view him as a beast.

Husbands, wives, sons, and daughters paid the cost of getting hurt and killed.

Today, some of us continue to display the American flag upon our chests.

Today, some of us continue to hope and pray that our nation has healed.

Our nation along with others in the world will miss those Twin Towers in the West.

Have we really pulled together as one?

Are we as far apart as we have always been?

One fact still remains, there is someone in the east looking at our way of life as a sin!

"Do Right Man"

She complains that her man never ever calls.

She looks out the window, paces the floors and beats the walls.

In the relationship, she gives all she can.

She constantly pleads with her God for a Do Right Man

She meets you and you call her each and every night.

But, she complains over and over that guys never treat her right.

You listen to every word as close as you can.

You are able to digest her total pain because you are a Do Right Man.

You realize that she has been hurt before.

You are aware that you did not cause that pain. Does she know?

You forgive her for no shows and non-returned calls. You are a Do Right Man.

She continuously explains to you how she gave that last guy her all.

You soon realize that is indeed the case and you should have read the writing on the wall.

So you stay and take all you can take.

No doubt, she wants you to pay for that other guy's mistakes.

You continue the attempts to please her in every way you can.

You realize after a period of time it's extremely hard being a Do Right Man.

"Unattached"

He enjoyed being attached most of the time. It really felt and looked okay in the beginning. As usual, he found himself back at square one as time progressed. He knows he should have asked more detailed questions in the beginning, but he felt [assumed -(ass-u-me)] He could trust his mate to tell him the important issues that would affect their lives. That was his problem! He knows he cannot love her and feels guilt pretending. He did not want to keep playing with her affections and he should not keep going through that guilt situation. He has reached a point in his life where it is possible for him to love for the first time in his life. In order for him to love someone he has to trust them in every way. He knows most people can forgive and forget, but he does not work that way. His only solitude is writing, he could not clear his head any other way. He had to accept his Higher Power's purpose, for him being alone and unattached at that time and at any other time in his life. He must trust his timing and remember, to everything there is a season, and a time to every purpose, including relationships. A good thing taken out of its appropriate season will be destroyed. If The Higher Power did not ordain a relationship for that time and season, it would lead to destruction.

"The World In, Which We Live"

How hard is it?

When will it get better?

The men that sit on their big powerful
horses astound me!

The slashing sound of their whips and
the loud commands quickly distract my
mind as though the noise is thunder.

There is a great heritage that we
must somehow rise above.

It is the tremendous amount of hate that has
hindered our Cities, States, and Countries.

Hate has arisen because of differences
in Religion, skin color and gender.

The belief in equality and living as one people
is not possible in the world in, which we live.

That possibility is far from reach!

It is as though we are attempting to force our minds through the neon fog in the air that hatred has made so thick that birds will not attempt to fly anymore.

The world in which we live has become susceptible to a disease that will not allow men to live up to their full potential.

It's sad but they never will, because of the difference in skin pigmentation, religious beliefs, and/or sexual orientation.

In order to build a better nation, we must rise above the built-in negative responses and prejudgments of others.

These prejudgments of others will continue to keep us in darkness, in the world in, which we live.

"The Why of Love"

Why is it so important to fight?

Why must we both be right?

Why is it so easy to look past love?

Why we can not see the pain and rise above?

Why is it so important for love to end as though
it operates on an unscheduled stop?

Why must we be the ones to always come out on top?

Why is it so easy to fall apart?

Why is there so much damage to the heart?

Why can't we deal with the unspoken pain?

Why are the loneliest days filled with rain?

Why can't we show the love that we truly feel?

Why can't we accept love in our lives
and agree that it is real?

*Why do we worry about love ending,
before it even begins?*

Why do we say, "I want to love you, but it depends?"

Why isn't it easy for us to see?

Just let love be!

"Fix It"

You can struggle with the question of life with a smile.

Go deep into your past and remember
things you saw as a child.

The hustle and bustle of things never made you quit.

You wish things were better in your
life and you want to fix it.

Your world seems unfair and unjust in the dark of night.

You're frantic, nervous, and in the mist of a terrible fright.

You can struggle with things of which you
haven't control or you can simply smile.

You tell yourself, "I must fix it."

You fail to see the growth in letting
yourself struggle for a while.

Give yourself a chance to rest in order
to return with a sharper wit.

You come to me and complain of the
world and all its troubles.

I remind you now as I have before. These issues are
the same as those of the Flintstones and Rubbles.

"He Was a Friend"

We met on a well-traveled road.

He said, "Hello", I also bid my ado.

Seemed O.K., it was the acceptable mode.

He looked not like me, nor perhaps you.

Later, I needed help in my despair.

It seemed impossible, but I was able to cope.

He appeared and my despair disappeared in thin air.

He gave me much more than hope.

"You owe me nothing," he said with a smile.

I thought to myself, I helped someone in the past.

My destiny seems closer now, not even a mile.

I have gone to so many places and oh so fast!

He and I grew up together; it's really sad.

This was so long ago, I can't say when.

Have I forgotten all the good that I had?

*I didn't recognize it at times, but
he's always been my friend.*

After a long road of trouble, it was clear to see.

The friend I so desperately needed turned out to be me.

"If It Is Meant to Be"

To obtain the true significance of life,
let us free ourselves and love something
greater than the act of loving.

If it is meant to be.

If we do not allow our life to bring
about joy and happiness

it will no longer bring about life.

If it is meant to be

Without fear, let us surrender our lives to a higher
power and be at peace with the outcome.

If it is meant to be, it will be.

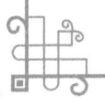

Just Let It Be"

I am missing you and you are missing me.

All we have to do is let it be.

I notice sometimes when you are not around,

I wish I could hug the image of you
that I have in my head.

I can smell the sweetness of your soul with
the profoundness of a bloodhound.

Our friendship will continue to grow even if we never wed.

I am missing you and you are missing me.

All we have to do is let it be.

I am missing you and you are missing me.

All we have to do is let it be.

Just let it be!

James M. McMullan, Ed. S.

"Love Is"

Love is filled with fear.

Love is a pain that comes in the dark of night.

Love can hurt someone who is near.

Love is filled with dreams dulling our sight.

We deny, we lie and we might even kill for it.

It comes with confusion, pain and despair, but we never quit.

When we are down, it lifts us up.

When we are up, it brings us down.

Love is good, love is bad.

Love is fun, love is sad.

Love is love, love is love.

Love is!

"Man What a Lady"

To be with her is compared to floating above ground.

When I think of her it makes me stop and turn around

I am at my lowest; almost under the gun.

I think of her for a second and life is fun.

I wonder if I will always feel this way.

Who knows?

For what will or will not be, who is to say?

That is the way it goes.

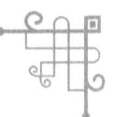

"Our Love"

Reaching for yesterday and
remembering the good things.

We played, we laughed, and we exchanged rings.

We promised to love each other forever and for a day.

As long as our love is meant to be, we will make a way.

The two of us will soon be three.

A boy or a girl, you can hardly wait to see.

For him or her and you, I thank the stars above.

Keep shining on our love.

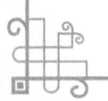

"Love Significance"

To obtain the true significance of love we need to free ourselves to love something greater than loving. If we don't allow our love to bring about joy and happiness, it will no longer bring about love. We need to give our will to a higher power and be able to live at peace with the outcome.

When I think of love, I'm reminded of my son as a small boy. He held his little puppy too tight because he did not want to drop him and hurt him. But he did not realize that he was hurting him by holding so tight. His puppy bit him and he dropped him. He looked at me with tears in his eyes and asked, "Dad, why did he bite me?" He didn't understand and at that time I did not have an appropriate response to his question.

Most people are scared of losing someone they love, and they hold on too tight, not realizing the pain that they are causing them. For that, they will be saddened, because they have damaged a special gift in the process. The special gift of love once damaged is often beyond repair.

"Love's Journey"

"If you ever know love, love will remain in you."

When you find someone, you truly love,
you become a different person.

When you find someone, you truly love,
your outlook on life changes.

When you find someone, you truly love,
you become someone new.

When you find someone, you truly love,
you become a better person.

When you find someone, you truly love,
you become someone happy.

When you find someone, you truly love,
you find a deep enter pace.

"Questionable Friend"

Are you really my friend?

You ask me to talk a certain way.

You beat me down every chance you get.

I feel as if my mind and soul need to mend.

Is it possible for you and I to see a better day?

It has been changing for the worst every since we met.

You insist that I hold up the standards of the good book.

As time goes on, it really does not matter,
because I have realized you are a crook.

James M. McMullan, Ed. S.

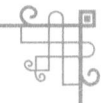

"What You Think"

You tell me how to wear my hair.

You tell me what type of shoes to buy.

You tell me to treat everyone fair.

You tell me to be an upstanding guy.

You tell me how to treat my daughter and son.

You tell me that when it comes to blessings, I have none.

I do not see how or feel that our lives link.

After all is said and done, it does
not matter what you think.

"Life"

Life is somewhat like watching a movie on television.

You are really enjoying it and in a relaxed mode.

All of a sudden, a commercial popped up.

Do you not find that annoying?

Well, I find that annoying also.

But I realize that in order to the entire movie and not miss a scene.

Just like life's journey, I must find interest in the commercials and watch them also.

"Come Back"

I feel myself drifting farther and farther away.

I reach out the paddle trying to hold on day by day.

I hear voices from a distance calling me.

The sounds are not coming in very clear.

Darkness is fast approaching, and it is difficult to see.

The liquid is rushing over and over against my ear.

The rescue boat appears to be floating out of sight.

I am trying my best to see the morning sun.

I keep drifting and drifting throughout the night.

If this water was not so deep, I would run.

Last night I remember being in my rack.

Last night seemed to be so far away.

I hear my mother's words, "Boy you gotta pray."

I hear her words while yelling at the ship,
"Come back, come back, come back."

"I Need One More Day"

When you love too much, walk away.

When you love too little, walk away.

When you hate too much, walk away.

When you hate too little, walk away.

When you hurt too much, walk away.

When you hurt too little, walk away.

When you see too much, walk away.

When you see too little, walk away.

When we are experiencing situations that we do not know what to do, walk away, just walk away to live one more day.

"We Sleep Alone"

We struggle with the real trauma as we sleep.

We lay in bed afraid of our dreams of despair.

We count through the night,
one sheep, two sheep, three sheep.

We find ourselves resting only to awake gasping for air.

We worry about the nightmares affecting our lover's rest.

We often sleep in another room to be our best.

As we worry about our gasp and a possible moan.

Time and circumstance allow us to sleep alone.

"My Last Duty Station"

It is always hard to get use to a place.

I am filled with the hustle at work as if is a race.

Getting used to the unit and all the new folk.

I did not realize it at the time, but I really missed Ft. Polk.

Things are very different here at Ft. Hood.

To my surprise, I have adjusted well,
as a real soldier should.

I found myself here after a short vacation.

As I have relocated over the years,
I always miss my last duty station.

James M. McMullan, Ed. S.

REFLECTION'S NOTE

REFLECTION'S NOTE

REFLECTION'S NOTE

REFLECTION'S NOTE

REFLECTION'S NOTE